desert heart

desert heart

diane roberson douiyssi

SHANTI ARTS PUBLISHING

BRUNSWICK, MAINE

Contents

drink deep from the well of courage

acknowledgments

I am deeply grateful to Kate Marshall Flaherty for lending
her brilliant, intuitive eye as an editor of this collection.
My intuitive energy work with Beverly Belling created an
incredible foundation for these poems. My friend and author
Mary Kay Shanley was an early supporter of my writing;
our chance meeting at the Ankeny library yielded a rich and
beautiful relationship.

I wish to thank the editor of the following publication in
which this poem first appeared:

Amethyst Review (November 2024): "ordinary"

fingers laced like a bride

choosing

i was lifted up and placed down
somewhere not of my choosing—

will i dart ahead in the dark, following everyone else?
or will i unfurl, a fiery light against gray sky?

~~a choice awaits~~
it is i who gets to choose

there is more

heart in
    your throat—
    you've hidden
    for so long
      you no longer
      know
         the sound of
your own voice—

      it is like
    a chickadee
      soft, insistent
    or   brash, raspy
      like a crow

      the pebble in
        your hand
        leaves
    no indentation
      you don't know
      it's there,
        insisting
that you awaken
    to your very
        self,
      the cotton sheets,
      the bark and flames,
      the truth
      you've been
      trying to outrun,
      but you don't feel
your bleeding feet

    one day
      a breeze,
        a freshness,

light and laughter,
will enter the room
and you'll
be drawn,
            you'll
recognize that
diaphanous mask
in another, see it
  shifted ever so
  slightly and
    answer that
    invitation—

      you, her
      here
      now—

      there's more,
      there's more to
        you, step
forward
  lift the silky veil,
      to see
            and be seen

grief

she shows up, hanging in the shadows,
unsure, unwelcome in the past, or scurried
away by flights of fancy, by everyday
drudgery, or shame. this time, i gesture her
in with a soft nod, she steps into the light—
her face ashen, etched with the sorrow of
lost moments, felled trees, pennies at the
bottom of a creek, silt covering or
carrying them away

she hesitates her slippers threadbare from
walking on the edges in the mists of sleep—i
offer her tea, a shawl and cushion

she sits, grateful yet silent, the clock ticks,
a crow caws and the slope of her shoulders
leans in weariness and she begins to speak,
of the losses, the time, the tears, the longings
ignored

finally spent, she sighs and looks upward—
a dove, gray, begins to sing a mourning
song

she looks at me

my eyes stay soft

beloved, it's all right—you're home—it's
time to rest. tomorrow the dawn will beckon
us both forward

the whisper

muddy tears
roll down
your cheeks
liquid pain
scathes
your skin,
sadness
etches
glass grooves
in your chest

the field
is empty—
save the
wind
whistling in
the nearby
grove, the
heat pulsing
off, rough,
an ache settles into
your hands

the sun
is high
baking the
clay,
your heart
hard

wait—
the tiniest
whisper
you almost
turn away

thinking it
a mirage

a string
plucked on
a broken
violin

you cock
your head
listening—
letting the wind,
raw and
jagged, pause
till
you hear it again—

your breath catches,
a bead of
sweat falls
between your
breasts
tracing
your
heart

yes—you
want to shout
run
leap—
but you wait,
expectant,
for this moonlit
call
to
draw your

                    feet forward
                    one after the
                other,
                    soles bare
        alone,
            yet echoes
                in the
                    wild

                        you're
                moving

tend to what's
important,
what glistens
what is
overlooked,
what matters—
leaves as they
unfurl, tiny
peach blossoms,
one bitter seed

tend,
to invite them—
shower your
attention
as
love—

a gentle rain
soaking
thirsty ground—
smile
touch
then set
them back, gentle,
these memories,
whole
healed
part of you
now,
cradled
a delicate gold
thread in
the cloak
of your
life

ordinary

you lay
down,
swirl your
fingertips
in the cool
stream—
surrounded
by water,
you want
to dissolve
into droplets,
melt into
brilliant sun,
diamonds in a
stream—
yet you
stay
clay,
heavy,
waterlogged,
waiting for
the flame
that will
turn the
wet dirt
into a
vessel
of light

the moon
is hiding,
the dark
howls—
you have to
quiet your
own thrumming
quaver to

hear the
whispers

i am here
too
i reside not
only in
the stars
or
the magic
of blossoms
or the
dance of
letters swirled
into gold

i am here too
among the
ordinary—
in the baked clay
that tastes
bitter as
it touches
your lips

i house the
unseen
miracles
of breath

come visit
me, i'll
spread a colorful
cloth, welcome
you in, welcome
you back
to your own
enchanted self

drink

bow your
 head, beloved,
  feel the life
   force pulsing
    around you—
     a red ripe
     raspberry
     on the vine
     for you to
       pick and
       place
          with
gentleness
          at your
             sweet lips
             let it melt—
                its tart
                sweetness
                   across
                your whole
               tongue,
               face,
               body—
                  lay you
                  bare in
                  that one
                  moist moment
       knowing
        all its
           glorious
             burst of beauty
             won't last—

                sink into
                  that
                knowing
                  and
let yourself
      go—
        lose yourself
         in this
              singular
                moment,
                its splendor
                   for
                   you alone,
               in this one
                   instant
  open
    yourself
         wide—
                and take in
             this
                feast lain
       full for you,
         only you,
          now—

go back

you're a small
  child once more—
  on a concrete
      sidewalk,
        scrabs of violets and
              dandelions—
              you run
              after your
              marble as
                  it
              rolls away—
reaching, searching
  the emerald
  grass, dreaming in that
  midday
      sun

you left
      there for
      delicacies designed to
      soothe—
        linen, ivory,
        cashmere—
      and for
      destinations intended to
      distract—
        marble bathrooms and
        gilded malls

don't you
  miss the
    air,
  full of
    pollen,

bees, the
sunlight
swirling the
      golden grains?

go back
   to what you
   knew in your
        10-year-old
        bones,
           to the
           hot concrete,
              baking its
                 warmth into
                    your scraped knees
go

into the night

you remember
the taste as
you stir
    the soup,
    look wistful
out the window
    the wind
 blows and
 your mouth
    recalls
 the sweetness
 of
  berries in
    bloom
the lick
  of juice
  that makes
  you cry
  out—

 yes,
   this

the lamp
 darkens
  and you
 wonder
 why you
 stay inside,
locked
  screens in
     place
       dust
      kept at bay

the light
fades,
but streaks
in the sky
are ribbons
that might
lead you
back to
joy

go out,
reach high,
grasp the
lilac-peach
strands,
fumble hand over
hand, stretching
into the darkness
through
doubt, confusion
fingers grasping

taste the
memories
of what
you loved
and let it
guide you
home

waiting

an acorn
tumbles
    from the
    arms of a tree—
bruised, chipped
     and forgotten
       on the
        solitary, dirt
        path,
         it encounters
        hot winds
          hustling
across
   the sands
dry, lonely
   arid—
winds blow,
    brittle leaves,
cracked and
      broken,
     swirl—

still
    the nut waits,
     knowing without
    knowing how,
    the moment will
    come—

      a gentle rain
      catches
   a spring breeze
    and the seed rolls
across grasses bending,
  the waters then
swell to a surge

so strong,
that all is lost
and the acorn
        is carried away
    again, to rest,
      on a carpet
      of blush
        rose petals
        dropped
            down,
momentarily, onto
        a bed of softness—

the golden lilt
  of sun and air,
        a sprinkle of
          dew, sinking
          deeper and
            deeper as the
        bed meets the
        earth and
          it begins to
              crack open—

not ready

your loss-
but-not-loss
lodges in my
drainpipe chest,
this thickness
choking my heart

your absence was
never anticipated—
although all candles
were plucked from frosting,
jokes of our birthday
songs sounding like
a dirge
should have made me
mindful,
should have made me
pay attention

the grief
of not being ready,
of having missed
the chance for a goodbye

violets hidden in
wax paper, pressed
pages of an old book—
their proud purple
faded to a tea-stained leaf—
are you still here?

i should have
laid shoes
near the door
i should have

been ready
i should have
cleaned the eaves
so the storm's rain
would travel
away
from drowning the mums,
guided to the grass

i never asked
you how to be, but
i didn't have to
because
you were there

maybe wondering
if you'd waited
too long
too

dusk

as the setting sun
wanes,
you look to your
achy hands
tired, idle
what are
they for
if
not to caress
soft cheeks,
pick diamonds
out of
dust?

a single tear
drops,
your heart
leans out,
does anyone
see?

let the quiet
comfort you—
the wind
carries whispers
for miles
across deserts,
oceans,
prairies—

let your
weary hands
fold in your
lap

fingers laced
like a
bride—waiting,
sparkling,
expectant, in the
here
now

acclimatizing

it comes,
 so often
  unbidden,
   perhaps a knock
   in the dead
   of night,
    or the bright
    white light
    of a long-
     hidden
     truth

     it
     thrusts
     you into
     a chaos of
      unmet expectations,
     of words dropping
     like lead,
     a heavy
     stone in the base of
    your belly
   lands, a ping
   of danger
    keeps your eyes
     open during the
     unending night
     your being
      longs to go
      back, back to
     before
     before you knew
    the truth of
    what was to come,
    the necessity
   of what was
  being asked

you thirst for
    the familiar,
      yearning in
          nostalgia for what
            once accompanied you

        never mind—

        draw on your breath,
        call on your beloveds,
        remember the star in
        your heart can be
        called forth—

the path may have
  loose stones or be
    uneven, your feet unsure,
      though soon enough as
        you move slowly, inexorably
          towards what must needs
          be, your step quickens,
        you no longer
        feel unsteady, because
      you look down
    and all you
  see are stars
    that have
      arisen to
        accompany you—
        constant, toward
      this new dawn
    this new
way

a candle in the darkest
pre-dawn moment

the calling

the first time
you heard,
  it was
  barely a
   whisper
a rush of
birds' wings
  a flutter
  of
   sunrise,
  but it
made you
      pause
place a
     hand on
     your
     heart

     then—
    called
     by the
    hands that
       clamored
   for you,
  the cries
  for help,
   the echoes
     of all the
other women looking
   elsewhere—
you
  slid away
  and you
   forgot
   what it
    felt like

but it
  visits you
     again,
     golden on
     a moonbeam's kiss
to your heart
            an ache
            that says
               yes, this—

     yet you
       sleep, the
             pillow is
   soft,
        it
   cradles
   your head
    in a familiar
embrace

  so it comes at
    night
      when the
    pews sit
      empty
      when the rain
      drops
on petals
      around
        dusky
         corners

    do you
      hear it?

        the moment

will arrive, quiet
one dewy
 morning,
 when you
 know the
time has
 come to
stop turning
      away—
         to dust the
              floor with
         a cloth,
         bring a
         cushion,
         and finally
         listen
         to the forest
         shuddering
            deep

      finally
       listen to
      the longing of
         the ocean,
         the wind,
            the
      peaks,
         to finally
            know there is
      nothing other
       than
               yes

all you've been given

all that you once loved tastes of salt,
bitter crystals line your tongue, grate
your teeth—your breath slows—
languid like a tiger, sun dazes, so
you hide your eyes afraid to see what
the slant of light illuminates laying
in tatters at your dusty feet. pick up
your cup to sip, to see the salt-crusted
threads—brilliant, and briny. touch
the strands of white, latticed cubes.
see what can be formed anew. what can
you make with these thickening crystal
cords—with all you've been given?

red

let your
  heart beat
with the
  crimson truth it
  knows

  dust, grasses
   sway in the
    wind under a
    scarlet
    sun

    your voice
   like an abandoned
    gem—a glint
     of ruby—
     opens
      the
      sky

set forth

put down your
satchel, heavy
  with the
    charred ashes of
  dreams revised
 smaller,
  perhaps abandoned, in
    the wake of your
    failures, or fears
    of being burned

    use your hands to
    touch the
        soil—
grazing fingers in
  the dirt that
  cloaks your
deepest core—
  sense a
 a way forward

        inside let kindle
      the fire to
    reach out,
      fanning that
      which you
        love—
          delight in what
            draws you
  nearer to this
    flush flame, to
    what gives
    you life, a
    breath, what
      embraces the warm
    skeins of love

look forward
  to the days
  that will come—
  and know
  you're here
    with purpose—
you're part
  of a bigger
    whole
a beautiful
  tapestry, a
    creation of
  love, an evolution
of humanity, a
    balm for suffering

  pick up your
brush, your pen—
  let them pour lines
  into this ache to
      connect and create
something that's
  needed,
    joyful—
  a swirl of light in
darkness—
  have heart as you
  bear it—
      yours but never
        yours—
  and then share—
      a profound sapphire
    drop
    in the wide
    ocean of the world

cradle

the light
   emanates from
   your fingers,
        a power
        to move
     others
        to
         tears
        to joy
to sorrow—
   to touch
   the cloak of
    a mighty
        oak,
        deeply grooved,
        that encases
       the truth
       in its
   every ring
      and in the
       acorns it
          scatters at
          your feet—

   will you pick
     up the pen
        with these fingers?
        will you
          share
what's golden,
     trapped in
   a net of
   beads, in
   the heart's
dream catcher—
     strands of

            sunlight
     ready to shine?

      you'll realize
      in a soft petaled
     moment, that
      these strings
      were never
        there
     to trap
      you,
        rather,
           to weave
       a cradle to
       hold your
           tender
           heart
     softly, so
        you can
           spread those fingers,
        reach to light
        a candle in the
        darkest
        pre-dawn
          moment, and
              give

     go love, the world
          is waiting

unwrapped

the words stop
at your parted
lips, your pen
   does not drop to the
      page, instead you
   close the notebook—
   whisked like an
empty husk—convinced of
      something other than
      the knowing
    that visits you
in the inky night
   sky,
that knowing
   that says your
   story is one that
must be told—your
words, strung together,
   gemstones on a gilded chain,
are a gift

remember—
once written, these jewels
     lay await in a
        sapphire
     velvet box—
a treasure for
another soul—
   a key to her
   unlocking a dream, to
       easing a clasp of
suffering,
   or to letting the
   still-small voice
   inside her be heard—
   as sonorous as a

cathedral's toll—
        i am okay, i will be okay,
        i matter

she'll pick up the offering,
        your lines become
    part of her life, her own
        story; and because
                she feels your truth,
                she will wrap these words
        like gems in
        a patterned piece of silk
        and place them to her lips,
            —a whisper, a
robin's egg, a coin —
                she will carry them,
        until she meets the
next soul, hungry or lost,
            with whom she will
                share these words

            when you close
        your eyes, you feel
        this running through your
    veins, and you remember—
            this desire to
        connect, to tell the
            truth as only you can

don't delay, don't
    doubt
    there are those
        longing to hear your
    voice, a cool quench
    on a desert dune,
        pick up your pen, smooth
    the pages of your heart, and
            write, your gift

at the stoplight—

the bus lurches—
she swings forward,
her uniform still
smeared with scarlet slashes
from the butcher's knife,
her feet still
icy
from the cold
metal vents she stood on—
a river of
blood below

she catches her step,
keys scratch the
flip phone, the one her
daughter can text
I am home
after she slides the deadbolt
back

it's 11 pm—
the other bodies on
the bus bored, faceless

she stares out the window—

a car, black, shiny,
glides to a stop beside the bus,
a blue screen whispers—
a whole world on that dashboard—
a hand with a ring on
delicate fingers
touches the screen—
it blooms like a burst
of colorful cotton candy—
sweet at first,

but in the heat
of the mouth, melts
to spun pastel strands—

all that's left is
saccharin grit

when i again forget what words can do[1]

when i again forget what words
    can do
        whisper in my ear:
        remember, beloved

remind me
    the sultry summer evenings, my
sister and i, with loose leaf,
crayons and construction paper.
july heat hot in our room, just us
writing ghost stories

remind me
    the composition notebook, tear-stained,
that kept me company,
far away from home,
    with ideas that felt foreign
at first, but turned curious,
with fascination

remind me
    the words that
    elicit tears or
    incite rage,
    that inform me,
        that make me lonely

when i forget,
    remind me how i
    trod to the mailbox, waiting for the
    blue and red of an airmail envelope.
my longing mixed on paper,
thin as an onion skin

when i forget again, what words can do
remind me of reading behind the veil in arabia[2]
and seeing
the women in oman, remind me
of poems that welcome,
speeches that become beacons

when i forget, say:
remember beloved, words will lead you home,
every time

1. Inspired by the final line of the poem "On a Day When I'm Sure Words Won't Make Things Better" by Rosemerry Wahtola Trommer

2. Unni Wikan, *Behind the Veil in Arabia: Women in Oman* (The University of Chicago Press, 1991)

amethyst

be
    draped in
        gold and
shining
    crystal orchids

each moment is an
        amethyst
            to be cracked
                open,
to perceive what
    is within

deep below
        the surface
                behind
the purple dust,
hidden
    small,
    see and it
    will bloom

turn it
    over,
let yourself
    glimpse
its glistening fissures

light the way

your fingers rest
        cool on the
        ivory page—
        the sheet beats silent—
        waiting
            for you to
                drop the
                cloak,
                pour your
                    heart out
                        and
bleed
   ache
   revel

so that others
        may find
          that still-small
                frightened
                part of
                themselves
                tucked
                    away—
    hidden in a
    wood trunk,
        under a wool
            blanket, or behind
              a window sheer—
          and coax it
                out,
                remembering
                  the sun on their
                    face, the
                        joy, the ache
                        underneath

every
        thing
they were
        ever given

    one wet drop
        of dew
        on their
        lips that could
    suddenly
        quench and
    reawaken a
        deep thirst
        for more
aliveness

    lick your
     dry lips,
        cracked in the
          sun,
        lift your hand,
                draw ink from
                the well
                    and light the
                      way

radiance

take heart young
     one—
   your life is
    laid out
  easy in some ways
  harder in others—
apples, persimmons,
bees all delight
  in the land,
and you trekked,
  homeless,
  untethered
    from community
  but not from the
     earth—

  dig your feet
  into the soil,
  dazzle in the
   sun—
  become a light
for others—
you'll gather
  them like
  moths dancing
  around a flame,
bewitched
  with
  your radiant
love

  they'll cry out
me, this is in
  me too—
  help, how can i, too?

you'll touch their
  wrist,
    unfold their fingers
          so they
  see in the
  palm of
    their very
  own hand—
  a rose petal
  open with
dewy promise—
  all they
  need to
      do
  is say yes

you'll watch
  them flutter,
  seeing their flight,
      all the while
      rooted
  in the glow
  you've never
    rested in
          before

time

minutes sprinkled
  like moon dust
    from faraway—
   you try to grasp
     them,
     molten bits,
     they slide
     from your hand
to the ground
     spent
     cooling—
     the fire inside
      longs to
      be breathed,
       the air
       fragrant,
        hot,
       barren

      grasp the grains
      of sand,
   pick them up
    let them sift
     down
     onto
      you
      through your
      words,
       spilling out like
        a quiet
   hourglass
    hidden in
     a tiny
      grove of
      palm trees

　　pick up the
　pen,
　　slash open the
burning bag
　　of desert dust in
　　your chest

　　　　　let it pour out, mix with
　　　　　those sand-minutes,
　　　　　a pool of glass
　　　　　formed at
　　　　　your
　　　　　feet,
　　　　　a structure
　　　　　beguiling, there
　　　　　for those who also
　　　　　long to turn its full shape

a heart kindled

whisper
  my name,
bend down
  and kiss the
dirt,
  your lips
  sandy,
  i step into
  your
  desert heart
    and
unwrap
  that ribbon
    that's tied
  you tight

    it slips
    away
      flutters in a
    damp breeze

    you
      step forward—
    dewdrops on
      your tongue,
      fire in your
            heart—
        and speak

taking flight

something
settles on the
edge
of your
awareness—
a hurt, an
unjustness, a
touch soft as
petals

you brush
it away,
with barely a
nod or
whisper—
it comes
back, becoming
a shape, a circle,
a penny
bleeding
drops of
copper
that turn
your heart
rust

still, you
busy
yourself
with threads to
gather,
soups to
stir, dust
to sweep—
and still
it calls

speak it
says
    cry it
says *rejoice*—

it offers
a basket of
    feathers
to flutter
at your
feet—
it grows in
your heart
and you,
poor unwitting
you, hold onto it
tighter, afraid
for a moment
of the weight
of this
coin,
until
it steals your
sleep
and aches
in your
copper-cold
bones

arise,
open
your mouth
and
speak,
what
you
know
to be
true

drink deep from the well
of courage

the sea

the sea that has
  pearls is far
too precious
to waste   spilling
  sloppy into a
   sieve
     to desalinate

the sea that holds
    forsaken pearls
    calls to me in my
    dreams:

    wake up and
    step outside,
    look for the ones
  hiding behind the
  swells—

  take their hands and
  leave through
the back door

  waste not, for
  the sun burns hot

   if you run quickly
     you may drop to your knees

and the tide will
  carry you

Inspired by the poem "The World" by Rumi, translated and performed by Fatimeh
Keshavarz for the On Being Project, 2012. Accessed 23 Oct 2023.
https://onbeing.org/poetry/the-world/

on our knees

can you not see?
i'm waving a flag in
red anger, in
white surrender, in
a pink rage for
all the women whose
tongues burn
from scorched shouting,
whose throats clench in
fear of reprisal,
who are not seen—
disappeared—

like the lost souls at the
plaza de mayo in buenos aires,
will our mothers look for us?

no, they'll shake their heads
softly, gray hair shorn, say
they tried to tell us— but we
wanted it all we said—
bacon and pans and
money and fame—
so their words fell like pennies
through a grate

we didn't listen, and they, with
their housecoats and curlers
and bone weariness,
waved us away

while we
yanked up expectations,
intent on remaking things

we never saw it coming—

the bitter backlash, the
way
absolute power absolutely
snaked into our skin—
—whispering
what they tell us
we need—the
yellow house with emerald
yard, royal blue china patterns,
and extraordinary children,
the clean glass desk in the
corner suite, successful side-hustles,
a joy-filled, purpose-driven, life

none of this means anything
while on our knees,
scabbed and scraped from
serving everyone—
but ourselves—

**

if we go limp, fall over in homage to the
earth,
would the world tilt
to right these wrongs?
would we see our mothers
and embrace them? glad
for their hands on our
shoulders,
for their arms
holding up
our very selves?

embark

whether the
night is
clear and your
path lit by
a sea of
jewels strewn
across
velvet indigo
or
whether
the fog
is thick
and impenetrable,
its dove-gray denseness
so heavy
it feels as
if you can't
breathe,
it matters
not
the size of
your steps
only that
you
move
like a trickle
of water
that slides inevitably,
unceasingly,
toward the
arms of the
sea
vast, wide
waiting

move toward
 that
 which
  calls you,
and
 fear not
the tremble
 in your
  heart or
   the tremor
   in your fingers,
 those shudders
  attest to
   the journey and
not
 your own
 divine
worthiness to
  set out

 light the
 lanterns,
  gather your
 shawl,
  kiss your
 loved ones,
  and
    fly
 home—

devoured

what is madness? is it counting carbs—a jail of food rules imprisoning us—yes, to broccoli and fiber—natural only—no, to fats—unless omega three or olive oil? is it crusts on our plates, tiny, medicated portions to ensure we're kept small—it is what it is—to keep checks and balances—what can i tell them—my daughters? who've inherited this prison made of shiny things and privation and pitched them into excess—we find relief in food, but furtively, daintily, doing what we need to comply—to be as expected—a red beach shovel on white sand   but somehow, we left behind the flesh of a peach, the melt of a slab of chocolate, or how we hold ourselves in this world, disdaining delight because it is all happening and no one stops to say no, this is not right— no one except the crone in the corner, gray haired, laughing in lusciousness, the raw blueberry juice on her lips—what if? what if we said nothing but abandoned this? walked out of this prison— one delicious bite at a time?

embrace

stand
  rooted in the
    soil
    dirt at your
      feet
    sure in
        your existence

    let the light
        dance in
            your soles—
create
    a basket
of your
      hands,
    cover
      the grasses
      with a
        blanket of
      brilliance,
        shore up
          those sheaths
          too scared,
      too small to
        unfurl

hold them
  with your
  silky, tensile
  strength as
      you look
      up
      knowing your
          face too is
            kissed by
              the divine

see the hunger
          in others
          as they regard
          you,
             whisper *it's*
                yours
                to own—
             your birthright

roots in
  dirt,
    strong,
       steady arms
    wide enough
    to embrace all
          the
             gifts
       and glory
          there is

to soar

      the orange, sweet
       word blooms
         on your
         tongue as
           if it's a
            slice of
              mandarin,
             a gold
                  droplet,
     a melt of
       sweet chocolate

         you lift it
          tender,
          cup the
          word and
          place it
         on the page
           where it
           swells with
            the clementine
            wings of
            butterflies,
          shimmering
           sands of a
           desert that
             hover above you

        you release
         it
         kissing it with
          a soft
          breath of
          longing
          before it

                    lifts
          from the open page
              to make its
                way into
                  the wind, to
              find the spiral ear
            of another's
                heart

listen—
     a joy, a sorrow,
   a permission opens
its wet wings
   and you
          stand still—
        watch it
              soar

the not-know place

she doesn't know
this place she's
found herself in
or
this strange
world where she
cries for lost pennies
and broken chairs left
curbside—

this place where she
no longer knows
how to dress—
her black pants too small
her gray tops too lifeless

this place where
words fly out of her
mouth and
others
raise eyebrows,
faces oh'ing like goldfish

this place where her
bones
settle,
she walks barefoot,
leaves the brambles
to overtake the yard

this place
where she
drinks water warm,
eats unpeeled
carrots and whole
packages of cookies—

where she sleeps as long as
she wants to, and,
    sometimes, stays up till
dawn—greeting the paling
    sky with wonder

it's no place she's
        known before—
        and yet—
                that's not quite true

        oh, her small hands
digging in dirt, her little feet
    running amongst the
tree roots, her rosy lips singing soft—

        they know—
this place is called home

Inspired by an invitation from the poet Peter Levitt to take his translation poem
and then "go to the place the poem takes you." Levitt, Peter. Und Zo. Facebook, 10
Dec. 2023, 9:23 a.m. https://www.facebook.com/peter.levitt.14/posts

be not afraid

do not be
  afraid,
do not
mistake this
  world
    and its slights
      and silver arrows
            as
            real

nothing
    is
real
  except that
  flame
    breathed into
      your soul
      from the
          divine—
      a mirror,
        guide-light
for those
who are
lost—

latch onto that
  elusive
    glass reflection
      for a
    moment,
        gaze
    into its infinity,
        taste its
            bitter tang
          and juice,
flickerings

that light
a fire
  in your
  throat
    to speak the

    tongues of flame,
  the words
once concealed,
    the truth
      the one

light under the door

it's late
night,
your eyes
flutter,
 the lump in
   your throat,
     sand
       lodged,
tears taste like the
 ashes
 of what
  you haven't
   done

   they fall
    as cinders on
    your delicate
      feet
  like orchids
    on a
    fire

so much
 beauty
  to awaken to,
    you push
    away the blankets,
      touch a well
        of night
          diamonds
          flung
           across a
      jeweler's cloth and
      move across

the room,
quiet
   stealth,
   others
   slumber
    but you've

    slept too
     long—

the imperceptible
  pull is
    feather soft,
      unmistakable, a
      strip of light
      at dawn
      through
      a crack—

      you, still
soft,
turn the
door handle,
determined
  to raise
  the only
   thing left
   inside
   your heart—
    your voice

do not look away

do not hide
your eyes
your lips
　　your face
　　　your heart,
you're here
　　　building—
　　　　with each
　　　　tender brick
　　　　you lay
　　　sand on your hands,
　　jewels ground
　　　to dust,
　　you set down one more
step on the bridge

do not stop
　reaching—
hearing the
　longing that
　arises—
　it is them
　calling
　you
　　　　your
　　　　heart
　　calling them

　　you've been gifted

words flow
　or colors
　swirl or
whispers caress—

your hands,
    heart, voice
       heals—

    reach out in
      love—
            don't
    let yourself
    drop to your
       knees—
          though the sun may
          beat, blister,
             the road, perhaps,
          will stretch out long

          but what you know
     in your
     own soft
     center,
        filled with
        sand-bleached mercy,
        is that
        you're being
        called—

     beloved,
      drink deep from
    the well
     of courage and
        carry on

lanterns

when
you lay
down   under
a fern   tree
clutching
your heart, anxious,
afraid—
remember
you are not alone—
you are with a
thousand other yous
who've lived before, who've
forged iron, swirled sand out of
murky streams, melted snow
on their hot tongues

you are not alone

but made luminous by
a thousand lanterns on the shore
of your life, lit by those who've gone
before—
mothers, sisters, souls in the night, in thin
but radiant houses, windows
buffering against the cold—

they left a light for you—a pinprick in the
dark void,
a luster
on an ebony tableau—

a star to light
your way
out of the shuddery
night

and into the
arms of the

one who loves you most—
yourself

the women before us

their feet
  stepped softly
      treading
        along the
    dirt
      road
    beaten down
      by those
    women who've
      traveled before,
        their early
          steps,
        tentative,
soft
    into unknown,
    the grasses
      rustle at
      their skirt hems,
      they've
      left the mind's
    pots and
        pans
  boiling over
on the
  stove

confused, people look up
        and feel
      an electric
        charge
        missing,
          a current
            hum that's
              suddenly absent

yet discomfort
  doesn't stop
      these women
from the
     journey
long and
    littered
    with those
who tried
  setting off
  before,
those who
got lost,
     blinded
  by rich promises
   of things would
   be different,
or swept up by the
 talons of
 others who'd
 pull them back—

  they've lived
   those lies,
   felt them baked in
their ancient
    bones laced
     with their
     own mothers' DNA

     do not stop
do not stop
    keep reaching
    out—find your
sisters' hands—

make a braid
of sweetgrass
woven tight,
so that
when you hear
the calls of
your soul on
that black
blue night—
you rise,
and find
your way

make haste

you come
  from across the plains
  and distant hills
  to seek,
    crossing rivers of
    doubt

time and again
    you've been turned away,
  petty scraps thrown
   at your feet,
     but this time the
       call is in your heart,
     your throat burns
     —and the winds are
strong at
      your back,
     your hair swirls,
      heavy robes cloak
    you for the
   journey
    you hear whispers of your
     former selves running
      in the trees,
      pine boughs
       bent,

        flitting
           among
          the silvery
      stars
         and you realize

      you've been on this
journey
     forever

but now,
  the time
  is urgent
sands fall
  as night
   sprinkles down
    onto the glass
     of your soul

      no time to sleep—
        make haste—
        make your
          way forward

  your breath
   catches
   as you see shimmers
   of what awaits
   in robes of stars and
    jeweled stone,
   your place with your sisters
    who also hasten—

      days stretch—
   a spindle of yarn—thin in
      places, yet thick enough to
        tell your story—

      make haste—
       your heart
       is calling you
         home

genesis

click
boom
in the aftermath
of the explosion
did the divine
catch their breath,
if only for a second,
the beauty and possibility
and fragmentation—
a million different
pieces
flung
far

did they
hope to
come together
again
a scintillating
ball
of light—

or
would they
remain scattered,
alone,
pushing
against one
another—
until—

a few
tattered souls
were drawn toward
each other, they move
a little closer, lend a lick
of warmth, a scrap of
comfort—

momentarily
buoying
amidst the
swirling

will
others see
and follow the
longing of their
souls to join?
to be one
again

 DIANE ROBERSON DOUIYSSI is a poet and writer currently living near the earth and peoples that nourish the world in South Dakota. She's a lifelong writer who received her B.A. from Grinnell College. Her poems have appeared or soon will appear in *Amethyst Review*, *Pasque Petals*, *song of ourself*, and *World Lives, Prairie Living*. She's founder of Inner Wisdom Wayfinding, where she hosts writing workshops and helps women who want to unlock their intuition and tell their stories.

Shanti Arts

Nature · Art · Spirit

Please visit us online
to browse our entire book catalog,
including poetry collections and fiction,
books on travel, nature, healing, art,
photography, and more.

Also take a look at our highly regarded art
and literary journal, *Still Point Arts Quarterly*,
which may be downloaded for free.

www.shantiarts.com

www.ingramcontent.com/pod-product-compliance
Lightning Source LLC
Chambersburg PA
CBHW021129070726
47591CB00014B/2081